T0011113

ANIMALS
Have Jobs

by Nadia Ali

PEBBLE
a capstone imprint

Published by Pebble, an imprint of Capstone
1710 Roe Crest Drive, North Mankato, Minnesota 56003
capstonepub.com

Copyright © 2023 by Capstone. All rights reserved. No part of this publication
may be reproduced in whole or in part, or stored in a retrieval system, or
transmitted in any form or by any means, electronic, mechanical, photocopying,
recording, or otherwise, without written permission of the publisher.

Library of Congress Cataloging-in-Publication Data is available on the Library
of Congress website.

ISBN: 9780756572006 (hardcover)
ISBN: 9780756571955 (paperback)
ISBN: 9780756571962 (ebook PDF)

Summary: Animals are busy! Sea dragon fathers care for babies. Eagle parents
build giant nests. Sea lions stand guard for one another. In every animal
community, animals have jobs to do, just like people!

Editorial Credits:
Editor: Kristen Mohn; Designer: Tracy Davies; Media Researcher: Svetlana
Zhurkin; Production Specialist: Katy LaVigne

Image Credits:
Alamy: Wildlife/Robert McGouey, 20; Dreamstime: Julian W, 13; Getty Images:
Adam Jones, 15, EcoPic, 24, Frank van den Bergh, 6, Gerard Soury, 16, Heinrich
van den Berg, 18, Jeff R. Clow, cover, Katherine Obrien, 7, KenCanning, 1,
10, Michael J. Cohen, 5, rusm, 11, Winfried Wisniewski, 14; Shutterstock:
abcwildlife, 21, Christian Nuebling, 19, Dan Olsen, 9, Daniel R. Cruikshanks, 27,
haseg77, 26, Hung Chung Chih, 29, Isarat, 23, Jo Crebbin, 22, Ken Griffiths, 12,
Leena Robinson, 25, Sergey Uryadnikov, 17, Svetlana Foote, 8, Udo Kieslich, 28

All internet sites appearing in back matter were available and accurate when
this book was sent to press.

Printed and bound in China 5132

TABLE OF CONTENTS

Words in **bold** are in the glossary.

Animal Jobs

People have many different jobs and **skills**. Animals do too!

Some animals look after eggs and babies. Others hunt or gather food. Some build homes or protect their families. Like people, many animals do all these things!

Babysit and Teach

Mama hippo looks after her **calf**. She feeds it and cares for it. The father hippo helps too. He stands guard. He keeps strangers away.

eggs

Sea dragons lay about 250 tiny eggs. The father's job is to protect them. He puts them under his tail to keep them safe until they hatch.

A mother alligator looks after her **hatchlings**. She gently holds them in her mouth. When the hatchlings are bigger, she gives them a ride on her back!

eggs

Surinam toads ride on backs too. A mother toad lays her eggs. Then the father puts the eggs on her back. The mother's skin grows over the eggs to keep them safe. In a few months, little toads pop out!

Up in the trees, a mother sloth looks after her cub. She gives it milk. She also chews plants to share with her baby. This is how the baby sloth learns what foods to eat.

A mother ostrich lays her *big* eggs in a *big* nest. Many ostriches share the large nest. Ostrich moms and dads take turns sitting on the eggs to protect them.

A father emu cares for his chicks. They follow him around. Chicks watch and learn as he finds plants and **insects** to eat. They whistle as they work. They whistle loudly if they get lost!

Hunt

Shhh! A mother tiger teaches her cubs to hunt. They spring upon their **prey** and bite the neck! When the tigers are full, they cover the prey. They come back later to eat more.

A pack of spotted hyenas may have
80 members! One powerful female is
the boss. She leads the pack on hunts.
Together they catch prey to feed their
families. Females and their young get
to eat first.

The cougar is built to hunt. Its back legs give the big cat power to run, climb, and jump. Cougars hide and watch. Then they pounce on deer, birds, and even insects to catch them.

An orca is an expert hunter. It swims after prey. The orca rams into the prey, then eats it for dinner.

Orcas also work in teams. They swim together to make big waves. Animals on floating ice above get knocked into the water. The orcas snatch them up.

prey

The Komodo dragon is the largest lizard. It is a big but quiet hunter. The Komodo may spend hours waiting in one spot. When it sees an animal, it lunges. Then the Komodo sinks its **venomous** teeth into its prey.

Build and Dig

The female leatherback turtle leaves the sea for a sandy beach. There, she uses her big back flippers to dig a hole. She lays her eggs and covers them with sand. Then she crawls back into the ocean.

Would you like to live underground? A chipmunk builds a **burrow**. It digs long tunnels. They lead to rooms for storing nuts, eating, and sleeping. The chipmunk gathers soft things to put in its burrow.

A beaver pair builds a house together. The beavers use their teeth to cut twigs and branches to make a lodge. Mud holds the lodge together. It's big enough for one family of beavers.

The male fiddler crab digs too. He digs a burrow in sand or mud, close to water. The burrow is used to stay safe, sleep, and **mate**. He will cover the door with sand to stay dry when waves come in!

A mother and father bald eagle share the job of building a nest. They gather sticks, twigs, and grass. They build it high in a tree. Year after year, they return to the same nest to raise a new family.

Bees buzz, and bees chew! They chew to make wax. It is a material like clay. They use the wax to build a **hive**. Each bee has a different job to help run the hive. They work as a team.

Guard and Protect

Meerkats live in big groups. They have different jobs. One job is guard. The guards stand on their back legs and watch for danger. They look for hawks, snakes, or other **predators**. If a guard spots one, it whistles to warn its family!

It is the mother squirrel's job to guard her young. When a predator comes near, the mother whistles. This tells the predator, "I see you!" The squirrel **flairs** and flicks her tail to scare away the predator.

Crows caw. Crows chase! In spring and summer, crows fight to protect the area around their nests. In the fall and winter, they fight less over **territory**. But they still fight over food!

Bark, bark, bark! Those aren't dogs. They're sea lions! Sea lions are loud and **feisty**. They **defend** their area from other sea lions. Mothers fight one another if their pups are in danger. They will bite to protect them.

Rhinoceroses are good at protecting themselves. These big animals can run fast. Rhinos aim their horns at an enemy and **charge**! Females use their horns to protect their babies. Don't get close!

Swan partners stay together for a long time. They protect each other and their babies. They honk, flap their wings, and chase anything that comes close. After they scare away a stranger, the mother and father celebrate with a dance!

Glossary

burrow (BURR-oh)—a hole or tunnel used as a home

calf (KAF)—a young animal such as a whale or elephant

charge (CHARJ)—to rush at in order to attack

defend (dih-FEND)—to try to keep safe

feisty (FYE-stee)—full of energy and attitude

flair (FLAYR)—to widen or make bigger

hatchling (HACH-ling)—an animal that has recently hatched from an egg

hive (HIVE)—a place where a group of bees lives

insect (IN-sekt)—a small animal with a hard outer shell, six legs, three body sections, and two antennae

mate (MAYT)—to join with another to produce young

predator (PREH-duh-tur)—an animal that hunts other animals for food

prey (PRAY)—an animal hunted for food

skill (SKILL)—an ability or knowledge to do something

territory (TAIR-uh-tor-ee)—an area of land that an animal claims as its own to live in

venomous (VEN-uh-muss)—able to produce a poison called venom

Read More

Everett, Michele Brummer. *Little Helpers: Animals on the Job!* Boston: Houghton Mifflin Harcourt, 2018.

McCann, Jackie. *Wow! Look What Animals Can Do!* London: Kingfisher, 2018.

Raatma, Lucia. *A Colony of Bees.* North Mankato, MN: Capstone, 2019.

Internet Sites

Ducksters: Animals
ducksters.com/animals.php

National Geographic Kids
kids.nationalgeographic.com/animals

PBS Kids: Animal Games
pbskids.org/games/animals

Index

About the Author

Nadia Ali is a children's book author. She writes in various genres and is especially fond of animals. Inspired by her kitty, Cici, she contributes pet articles and features to magazines and websites. Nadia was born in London and currently resides in the Caribbean, where she happily swapped out London's gray skies for clear blue skies. She lives with her husband and has two married daughters.